Praise for All These Ghosts

"Silas House is a southern institution, and his first collection of poetry is heartbreaking in all the best ways. You'd be hard-pressed to find anyone who loves the South more while continually working to understand its history and untangle its present."
—Jason Isbell, Grammy-winning singer-songwriter

"An author I reliably depend on to represent our home with respect, beauty, and authenticity. I love the sense of pride that comes through in so many of these poems."
—Barbara Kingsolver, author of Demon Copperhead

"I never met a Kentuckian who wasn't either thinking about going home or actually going home: I've read that on more than one poster back home, and if you're kin to the land and the people there, then, well, you know. But what I didn't know until reading Silas House's poems was just how that aching lonesome began, even in childhood as I, too, 'was already grieving the passing of all I knew / and loved.' Harder still is the solastalgia—that kind of homesickness while still at home—that grows as you grow up, or as he puts it, not homesickness but 'timesickness,' grieving a home lost to years as well as to floods, an Appalachia washed away by thoughtless development and acculturation alike. All These Ghosts then is a kind of elegy, but like any lament worth its salt, it's equally praise song—to soup beans and cornbread, to barefooted nights loud with insects, to those who have carried us through all that loss, and—just as Silas has done for me though this joyful, tender collection—carry us still."
—Nickole Brown, author of Fanny Says

"Throughout this marvelous collection House brings a finely tuned and thoughtful seeing to every poem. As he describes a first touch of hands with a friend who 'never came out,' we witness behind the 'green curtain' of a waterfall 'a small moment / of ecstasy . . . akin to drowning.' Such close attention is as perfect as the Hopkins poem to which House pays tribute in his epigraph. I was not surprised to find this acclaimed novelist spinning narrative poems that enthrall, enchant, and sometimes break your heart as in 'Behold This Dreamer' where the assault of a gay man is retold with stunning veracity and conviction. There are lyrical poems as well, possessing the same close attention to place and character found in all his work, thus making this a supremely impressive collection. In another poem we read: 'Come here, and rest. Let me help you.' These poems most certainly will do just that and more. I can only give thanks we have as fine an artist as Silas House to share his wisdom in poems of such beauty and power."
—Marc Harshman, Poet Laureate of West Virginia
  and author of Dispatch from the Mountain State

"Early in Silas House's poetry collection *All These Ghosts*, the landscape is set so beautifully, so skillfully, so convincingly, that I carried the Kentucky mountains and its people with me as I turned every consequent page, feeling the accumulation of love, and love's losses, as if watching a wild onion grow, that ancient symbol of complicated but natural love. There is Wordsworthian eloquence in Silas House's impressive and gorgeous poetry debut. What a gift to readers everywhere."
—**Kathleen Driskell**, Kentucky Poet Laureate 2025–26
    and author of *Goat-Footed Gods: Poems*

"To read this book is to be carried along by story and song, by ferns and dogs and water and language. 'This is my tongue for you, / whispering our history: words words words,' House assures the reader, and even as these poems grieve over the death of loved ones, over environmental devastation, over 'timesickness,' over our country's embrace of fascism, they also ground the reader in a deep and abiding love of that place, of kin, of the 'little fire' that lights the hearts of all the 'everyday people who / keep the engine of the world / running.' *All These Ghosts* is deeply Appalachian in its plainspoken honesty, its heartrending use of narrative, and its subtle use of complex form. 'Do not truck in empire,' it advises. After all, 'God lives in between / the pages of books.' In the mountains there is 'a secret cathedral / made of wildness.'"
—**Annie Woodford**, author of *Where You Come From Is Gone*

All These Ghosts

All These Ghosts

poems

Silas House

BLAIR

Printed in the United States of America

Cover design by Laura Williams
Interior design by April Leidig

Blair is an imprint of Carolina Wren Press.

*The mission of Blair/Carolina Wren Press is to seek out, nurture,
and promote literary work by new and underrepresented writers.*

We gratefully acknowledge the ongoing support of general
operations by the Durham Arts Council's United Arts Fund
and the North Carolina Arts Council.

Library of Congress Cataloging-in-Publication Data
Names: House, Silas, 1971– author | Kingsolver, Barbara interviewer
Title: All these ghosts : poems / by Silas House.
Description: Durham : Blair, 2025.
Identifiers: LCCN 2025020415 (print) | LCCN 2025020416 (ebook) |
    ISBN 9781958888698 hardcover | ISBN 9781958888759 ebook
Subjects: LCGFT: Poetry
Classification: LCC PS3558.O8659 A78 2025 (print) |
    LCC PS3558.O8659 (ebook) | DDC 811/.54—dc23/eng/20250521
LC record available at https://lccn.loc.gov/2025020415
LC ebook record available at https://lccn.loc.gov/2025020416

Contents

Dedicated to Sandra Stidham,
my seventh grade English teacher,
who read us poems

Lost Place

After A. E. Houseman

I hear a song that kills yet is a hinge
from my country so far, so close:
What is that green remembered ridge,
what trees, what pastures are those?

I float above crowded porches and tables.
All these ghosts, just beyond my reach.
I would love them more if I was able
to go back in time and believe.

I recall the wild places, fecund, rich.
I wade into the creek, diaphanous
myself, am I haint or witch?
Listen to me: Once here was happiness.

Now, this is the land of the beguiled,
I see it before me so plain,
the little paths I trod as a child
and will never mark again.

Part I

Gloaming

There is a cool that often moves over the mountains
in the evening. The day eases away, so secretly
no one notices until it is gone. Peach light
     steams along the horizon,
changing the shape of things. Night does not
give a hint of arrival and for a while,
     there is just the cool,
when there is no dark and no day, stretched out like ice.
     No clocks ticking
the minutes, no movement of the earth,
nothing growing or changing.
This is the gloaming
and the cool peaceful, soft. Mist
seeps out of the jagged cliffs like ghosts.
The breeze stirs the trees, dampening thirsty leaves.
No night sounds are heard. One bird hollers
far up the mountain and its lonesome
cry cracks the stillness. The crickets and katydids
and all the little live things begin their prayers
in the trees and grasses, on creekbanks where
the water slips over mossy rocks.
     The kudzu exhales and rests.
     The wild grapes offer their scent
to the twilight. This is an evening like that.

Two men work side by side in their garden,
chopping out the weeds that grow
most rampant in high summer.
     No one sees them briefly touch hands.
Boys lean into the mouths of their cars with grease
smeared up their arms and across their bare
chests, their shining tools lying at their feet.
Young wives sweep the porches or break
beans. A woman picks dead petals
from her plants, singing under her breath. Children

must be called in from playing. They smell of sweet sweat
and the ridge spine, of leaves and dirt and mossy rocks.
Their shoes are still damp from stomping
            through the creek.

A woman stands at the kitchen sink, finishing
the supper dishes, lost in thought as she looks
out the window. A darkening yard. Lightning bugs
drift up from the ground beneath the oldest trees.
            What happened to the girl she used to be? She doesn't
            recall her slipping away. A whippoorwill
sings. A hoot owl gives up its shivering cry. A mother
fox creeps out, sees that the shadows are falling,
and ventures forth to hunt. She will carry food
to her babies who are already sleeping,
far back in the den. A bobcat stirs,
            green eyes glaring over the hills as the western
            sky purples into complete darkness.

My people on their porches, living
in the cool of the day. They love this place
even when they don't. They have dreams
just like you. But no one ever thinks about that.
This is what it was like when I was a boy,
when the world was young and I believed
nothing would ever change. In the gloaming,
in the cool of the day, before I lost my people,
and before I lost my place in the sweet old world.

Blues

I.

Where I'm from we paint porch ceilings
haint-blue. A pale, soft color that keeps
spiders from building their webs there,
thinking a lovely sky looms where
they need shelter. Legend has it
the color scares off ghosts, too, but
that never worked for us. We lived
with the past breathing down our necks.

II.

I've never seen a whippoorwill
but I heard them often as a child.
Years now, since I've heard their pining
call. Often in the night I stand
sentinel near the creek, waiting
in the hopes they might testify,
singing their melancholy blues.

III.

The blue hour is the quiet
time not long before dawn. Witches
glide down from the high rocks and peek
into our windows. The dead walk
the country roads under starless skies.
There are panthers in these mountains
that sound like women screaming when
lonely in the long-legged night.

IV.

My aunt kept four pieces of blue
Depression glass in front of the
western window so they could catch

the last light of day, easing
across the floor and up the wall,
painting her face cerulean,
always closing her eyes before
the luminescence reached them.

V.

We used to listen to Joni Mitchell
wishing for a river,
recalling Little Green, dreaming
California, singing *shampoo you*.
But most of all, mourning for Blue.
We danced and sang along while we
washed dishes or sat still: me—you.

VI.

Once, our desire so tremendous,
we pulled the Vespa to the side
of the road, slipped into leaf-light
woods and tore at our clothes, ate
each other's lips like cherries, laid
on the bare ground and once spent
we saw the sky, alive and aching,
stretched above us like an ocean.

VII.

The first thing I saw were her eyes,
the color of anemones,
the way I imagine waters
of the Mediterranean.
I have not seen the sea nor do
I need to now because I can
see the world in her face.

VIII.

One day I knew what *the blues* meant.
The whole world shifted yet never
righted. All things have a color
and grief is blue. The ache you feel
when you realize it will not fade,
nor darken. Nothing lasts for me
or for you. Not even the blues.

Easter 1954 (Sis)

She would rather climb up to the high rocks,
but her granny only pleaded with her once a year
and at night she lay awake listening to the clocks so
she cannot refuse her, who has sewn this delicate
white dress special for today. The lovely hang
of skirt. Small capped sleeves and frill down the
front. All white, even the round, cloth buttons.
On the porch her grandmother is waiting,
drinking black coffee, singing
> *I love to tell the story*
> *because I know it's true.*

She only feels that way up on the mountain
> when the trees become still
in the purpling of evening. Well, she is wearing the dress
for her granny but she must be herself.
> She eases on red lipstick, has not removed the
> nail polish as requested. She ties a thin ribbon
> in the center of her collar, cardinal-colored,
> slips on red heels, pinches pink into her cheeks.

Outside the old woman says *Lord, honey* and laughs.
They lock arms and stroll along the creek
toward the thrumming church, lavender of redbuds
and lace of dogwoods decorating the hills on either side.

My Mother, Orphaned at Ten

I do not like to think of her alone
in that dark moment after they told her
yet I have been picturing her my whole
life. She was little and surely afraid.
A cold day for May, rain falling aslant,
gray sky hunkered low over the graveyard,
and growling. She might have clutched a doll but
no, was too poor for that. Then she grew up.
Working, busy, fast, determined, her hands
bleach-shriveled, her mind set on survival.
She learned lovely penmanship and typing.
Always smiling despite her crooked teeth.
Don't ever give up, she sometimes whispered
to herself when all was lost. Now she says
when she felt me shiver in her belly
that was the first time she ever was full.

Sis, 1956

Her son's little hand in hers as they stroll the midway with the barkers hollering at the Leslie County Fair. Every man they pass winks at her, or whistles, or blows a kiss. One of them says *Mmm Mmm* as if he has just bitten into her. On the Ferris wheel the metal car sways in the hot August night. The town below them. The mountains, beyond, an endless sea. The moon is so alone. She can feel the blues moving in. When the ride is over the operator unlatches their car and lets his eyes run down the length of her. He is sucking on a dirty toothpick; his lips are red and small. He offers his hand but she ignores it so he says *Bitch* under his breath. Two men on a rickety stage singing *You're running wild, how long can this go on?* She and her son walk through the pastel lights being cast by the Merry Go Round. She is buying candied apples when the man presses himself against her, his breath hot on her neck. *Want some of that, honey?* His whiskied mouth is a smudge at her ear. She plucks the pearl-handled knife from her purse as if picking a berry, flicks it open with her thumb, pivots to nudge the small clean blade against the pulsing vein in his neck. The man looks down at her in amazement until she relents, turns, and sashays away.

She will not give him,
or anyone, the pleasure
of her glancing back.

Not Shown in the Picture of
My Father Being Baptized in 1958

The summer sun, so hot he could hear it
burning the sky above them. The thirsty
leaves, in bondage to the endless August.
Women in daffodil dresses singing
Then sings my soul my savior God to thee.
Smooth rocks on the river's floor, eternal.
Tips of willows parting the smooth surface
while the frogs and insects wait to commence.
My granny's eyes, not facing the round lens,
her rough hands clasped in front of her, praying.
The doubt in his heart that would always be
thrumming there, present as the warm water.
But O! the thrill of hope when he was dunked,
the cleanness of that moment, the freedom.

Only Thing He Ever Gave Her

Never knew her daddy, never gave a damn
either, she'd say, drawing hard on her cigarette,
ember brightening. Did, though. Did.
      When she was big with her first child, word came that he
      was nigh death. She knew where he lived. Always had.

See her powder blue Falcon racing
the crooked road through Rockhouse, passing
Owl's Nest and Hurt's Creek, past Avawam and the mouth
of Laurel Branch, on through Happy Valley.
Off the blacktop now, gravel, then dirt, dust
billowing behind her, until she reached

Grapevine. Mountains steep as calf faces,
high summer and the smell of wild grapes
caused her mouth to water. At her father's house
dozens of tomatoes stood in line
on the porch railings, from a hard green all
the way to a bursting red. She grabbed the ripest
one and bit into it like an apple, savored
the magic with her eyes closed. She knocked

and his old woman showed her to the shadowy
bedroom where he was propped, gasping for breath,
      grasping for her hand, and the odor
      of rotting lungs thick on the heat. She held
      his gnarled fingers, listened while he apologized.

Back outside, she found a cardboard box
and gathered all the tomatoes. She glanced
at them, propped there on the backseat as she steered
the treacherous curves toward home.

In her kitchen she boiled the ripe ones,
skinned them, mashed them to juice. Just as she turned
the lid on the last jar her water broke.
     Sometimes on blue days long after the baby
     died she'd stand in the root cellar, watching
     the jars. Red and pretty as blood. Untouched.

What She Missed

Daddy took me to see Loretta Lynn
at Cumberland Falls but my mother,
mesmerized by the Pentecost, believed
country music was a sin. Loretta
wore a long gingham dress and smiled the whole time
she sang about beating up women, or men,
and being a coal miner's daughter,
like my own mother, who was at home,
praying. Later she would lament
how much she missed, would grieve
about how she never took me to movies
or a carnival, how she spent Halloween
in the church basement with children dressed
as John the Baptists or Bathshebas while my
cousins took me trick or treating. Once, they
made me up like Dolly Parton. Folks laughed
because they could see I was a boy. One
old man said, "You got some big titties there,"
and dropped a whole Hershey bar into my bag.
My cousin steered me away and called
him a pervert. Many years later I realized
he was talking to her, not my
costume. At the Loretta show my father
smoked and didn't sing along. A man thanked
him for his service because he saw his tattoo
from Vietnam. When the show was
over he carried me through the crowd
on his hip even though I was too old
for that by then. I felt taller than
I ever had before.

My cousin took me to see *E.T.*
I wanted to cry so badly but knew
that boys were not supposed to, then I heard
the sobbing around me and I let

the tears drip down my face. I had never
been so bereft. Never, except all the
times I wanted my mother to be with us.
When John Anderson came to sing
at the Falls my aunt took me. People were
crazy about him back then, the radio
playing "Just a Swingin' " a dozen
times a day. When he sang that song
everybody clapped and hollered. My aunt
leaned down and whispered in my ear
He's ye people. We're kin. A couple
was dancing down front, the woman twirling
beneath the man's hand like the ballerina
in my mother's jewelry box, the one
who popped up and began to dance
when I opened the lid and set her free.

First Home

We lived in a little red and white trailer
near the banks of Robinson Creek.

Metal screen door's screech, brown paneled walls,
bedrooms safe as wombs.

Sandbox, beagle, the porch floor's concrete cool
and solid.

Wooden table, four chairs. My mother there, worried
with checkbook, singing

to the radio. *I Was Country When
Country Wasn't Cool.*

Soup beans, cornbread, chow-chow, grilled cheese, pickled
baloney, saltines.

Blue TV glow in a darkened room: *The
Waltons, Little House.*

Winston Lights, peach Nehi, bottles of Stroh's.
Solitaire, Rummy.

The women laugh, wash dishes, hips touching.
Men build a gnat smoke.

Music from the church next door. Feet stomping,
hands clapping, drums.

God.

I went with my daddy into the woods
to dig a dogwood

he planted in our yard. I hope the
    tree grows there today.

I am a long way gone from that place, yet
    marked by it, still. They

called us trailer trash, but oh, how sweet rain
    sounded on its roof.

Cornbread

I like to scoop the meal up by hand,
no spoon, so I can feel the grain
on my fingers, wonder at the fields
that gave it life. I love the splash
of egg, the gallop of buttermilk.
When I mix all of this I see
my mother cooking for me after
a long day bent over stoves, spent
serving all of the mean children
at the Lily Elementary School.
I see my aunt, cigarette
planted firmly between her teeth
as she holds the bowl against her
belly, eyes on *The Young and the
Restless* while the cast iron skillet
of grease heats in the roaring gas
oven. I see my grandmother and
every woman before her
in my family and yes, even
the occasional man who lowered
himself to cook, who secretly
enjoyed fingering the meal.
And here I am, too, timesick
once again. If I could go back
I would tell my mother to go,
sit down, and rest. I would memorize
every word my aunt said
as she taught me how to cook, how to
live in this world, how to be
myself. I would kiss Mamaw
on the forehead and spend time
with her at her little wooden table,
savoring every bite, listening.

I'd ask Granny to tell me that story
one more time, please.
This is the curse of who we are
as a people, always eating
our own history, tasting the past.

Boy in the Bubble

Six years old, two weeks spent in a croup tent.
Plastic sheets, the constant wheeze of the machine
meant to help me breathe.

My mother refused to leave, unable
to rest while she listened to the heave
of my strangled chest.

That whole first year of school I was sickly, struggling
to seize enough air, a puny boy,
smothered and frail.

They plunged needles into me, counted blood
cells. The whole church squeezed in my bedroom,
prayers gasped and yelled.

Speaking in tongues, cries released at fever pitch,
arms held high. My forehead anointed with oil,
preacher's spittle on my eyes.

I inhaled their incantations, my faith
sighed in my veins, as light eased
the darkness of my lungs.

At the Opening of *Coal Miner's Daughter,*
Corbin, Kentucky, March 27, 1980

A line snaked down the sidewalk
all the way to the grocery store.
People stomped their feet to stay
warm and plumes of white puffed
out of their mouths. When snow started
falling a little murmur of joy
escaped the crowd. My aunt, Sis,
was not fazed by the cold.
She drew hard on her Winston and eyed
me, leaning down. Blue eye shadow,
chipped fingernail polish, hands worn
by waitressing and too much loving
and factory work. "Are you froze
to death, baby?" Yes, I was. I didn't care
if it *was* Loretta Lynn. Why
did we have to wait so long anyway?
Sis plucked the cigarette from her lips
and looked me right in the eye.
"Because," she said, "she's one of *us.*"
Before that I had never known there was an us.
But ever since the world has been divided in two.

Porches, Early 1980s

I.

My ear against the concrete
floor, I breathe in the roses;
I want to eat them. My aunt
and cousins are smoking and
laughing. *Everybody*
knows she's one of them lezzies.

II.

Sweet tea sweats in a Smurfs glass,
a glistening meatloaf steams
on my plate. I've always loved
my mother's hands. *Now, I know*
Michael is like family
but I don't want you ever
to be alone with him. Do
you hear me honey? Listen.

III.

My sister and her boyfriend
are swinging so high their feet
almost touch the cool haint-blue
ceiling. She has torn down a
spider's web and is teasing
him with it but his gray eyes
are on me. *Why's he set like*
that? he asks and she doesn't
understand so he explains:
Like a girl. And talks like one.

IV.

Granny has her own rocker
and nobody better sit
there. She swats at flies and zips
a stream of tobacco juice
into a Coke bottle, stares
at me. *What're you gonna
be when you grow up? Yourself?
Or like all the rest of em?*

Lunchlady

Always in the blue hour my mother
arose and dressed while the eastern sky cracked
like a bloody egg. Chafed hands forever
paled by bleach, an eternity of scrubbed
dishes, ready to catch whatever my
father threw our way in a fit of rage.

I did not understand the moment of
darkness before she flipped on the lunchroom
lights. I never witnessed the burn of grease
nor felt the prick of broom handle splinters.

Many of the children never saw her
offer them food. For others she rendered
the lone tenderness in their long days.
I thanked her, but not enough, now or then.

Cousins

Oh, we were wild back then
we drove fast and danced hard
me and my cousins
we laughed with heads thrown back

we drove fast and danced hard
fiddles sawed, guitars plucked
we laughed with heads thrown back
workin' on some night moves

fiddles sawed, guitars plucked
arms thrown over shoulders
workin' on some night moves
young and unafraid

arms thrown over shoulders
we loved each other so
young and unafraid
all the world was ours

we loved each other so
oh, we were wild back then
all the world was ours
me and my cousins

His Body, Appalachia

When he lay like that
his legs made the shapes of steep
hills. His veins were the same
as rivers. Like leaves.

His groin was a shady
place with a warm spring.
In his armpits were orchards.
His belly was a wide

valley. If he rolled
over and arched his back
just so, his spine became
a ridge and his rump

rounded hills. His heart
was a rocky cliff.

Cumberland Falls

O, let them be...
—Gerard Manley Hopkins

In high school the biggest dare was to slink
over the slick rocks flanking Cumberland Falls,
where the wide but shallow river dives
seventy feet into a deep pool of froth.
There, people say, catfish big as men twist
and slither, awaiting suppers sped
their way. You can see a rainbow at night,
shimmering on the mist during a full moon
and a clear sky. This is true. I snuck
behind the green curtain once with my best friend,
whose name I won't say because he
never came out. Just as we reached the veil
of water where we would disappear
into another world, I slipped. My right leg
slid down the cold boulder and before
I could plunge into the churning chaos
where torrent met river, he grabbed hold
of my hand. I was so electrified
by his touch I didn't think of how close
I was to being swept away.
Instead, I thought how a small moment
of ecstasy is akin to drowning.
He held on for a beat longer
than necessary. The roar behind
the falls was a deafening symphony heard
only by those brave enough
to penetrate this darksome cavern
carved by centuries. Fern-laden, alive
with the smell of moss. A secret cathedral
made of wildness and wet. We were mesmerized,
and stood watching the cascade as if frozen
yet, as if we might see through to the other side.

Dale Hollow Lake, 1989

On the green water
    the floats bobbed
red as candied apples
    and I believed we would always be like this,
my cousins, singing together
    as we drifted on the lake
with our parents no longer watching
    from the bank.
We were teenagers now,
    as wild and free
as we would ever be,
    ribbons on a breeze.
But this was before
    marriage or babies
        before presidents
made us choose between
    each other and dreams
        of what could be.
All of life was a carnival
    then, bright lights
        and twirling rides.
We held onto each other
    as our legs kicked the lake
and sang along
    with Tracy Chapman:
        I had a feeling that I belonged.

Bandit

A prayer for the wild at heart,
kept in cages.
—Tennessee Williams

My uncle kept a raccoon in a box
to see if it could break out. When escape
neared he added more barriers, watching
its desperate attempts and bloodied paws.
In the black February night I laid
awake, imagining the stealthy fellow,
frostbitten. I worried there were others
like him, suffering alone and afraid.
I crept in the blue light before morning,
unlatched the door, and the bandit scampered
away on sore, silent feet. I waited
twenty years to tell it because I was
afraid of my uncle's wrath. But always
I have that moment of seeing freedom.

Watch Closely

You
can learn
all you need
to know about
someone by watching
how they treat small things.

Decapitation

She wouldn't hush until I killed
the black snake who was living
beneath our back porch. I could have
told her no, could've shouted
the word. Instead I fetched the hoe
from its leaning place, a slice
through the August air and then
the deep gouge into wondrous
neck revealing a bloom of blood
and a diaphanous layer
of muscle. Still the snake lived
and I brought the hoe down again
until the head was severed. When
the killing was done she stepped back
into the air-conditioned trailer
to read her magazines
about southern living and I
was left with the body. This
is how it always happened,
you see. *It was only trying*
to survive, I said, to no one,
to the blistering summer sun.

Three Sisters

III.

I had been gone from home twenty-three years
when I learned that Michael Burns had been killed.
He was showing his kids how to dive from
the Third Sister, but had misjudged, his head
split open against the wet rocks below,
his body sinking down to depths colder
than cold in the lake he'd known his whole life.

II.

Six boys about to graduate high school,
midnight drunk, undressing on the Second
Sister despite the full moon. I tried to
not look at the muscles in Michael Burns's
back. One by one we ran, plunged into air,
Laurel Lake taking us, warm as a bath.
Our laughter echoed down the cove, foxes'
ears made alert. We climbed back up and he
caught me looking that time but he just smiled
and punched my arm the way a brother might.

I.

I was little, swallowed by my orange
life vest. Trinity of cliffs, one higher
than the next. My older cousins had sliced
through the air like perfect knives, were bobbing
now on the green water below, urging
me on. My father waited in the boat,
sunburned and tired. My fear was made larger
by the chanting, my shame blooming as they
climbed up to go again. But then I saw
the look on my father's face and although
I was afraid, I stepped forward, and jumped.

Little Fire

I was always so afraid of being left
behind. I was sure the Rapture
would take you all in the Twinkling of an Eye
and strand me. Because I questioned
too much. Sometimes I doubted.
Often I pined for the lost boys
who sat petulant, aflame on the back pew.

One day the wrath was too much so I escaped.
I wandered for years, an Israelite
in the wilderness. Not one of you offered
shelter. I stood on your creaking porches
with a suitcase at my feet, staring
at the closed doors. I heard the clocks
striking seven inside. You watched
from the curtain's edge, holding your breath.

      I had nothing

but little creeks and trees
to comfort me. Dogs, books, music, mountains.
I found a family when blood left me in the cold
night, but somehow, I kept myself warm.

All my life you've told me I'm no good.
You've said I am not worthy
of God's love. But there was always this

      little
      fire

burning in me,
and no one ever could put it out.

Inanimate

A pristine sewing kit, not much bigger
than a matchbook, tucked away in my dead
aunt's round cookie tin. Lid decorated
with blue roses. Compliments Rainbo Bread,
1958. Six silver needles.
Seventy impatient years measuring
time, waiting for this moment when I would
slide one out of the gold foil rectangle.
The ecstasy of red thread finally
present in eye. The yelp as it pierces
the fabric, sweet singing as the needle
performs repair. Even the smallest things
might spend decades feeling unimportant
until one day, when least expected, joy.

Drought

Finally: rain, after three months of dust
coating the waxy tulip poplar leaves
and tiger lilies standing muted, so
pale in those miles of Kentucky ditch-lines,
orange reduced to the ghost of orange.

A gray fourth of July and all the lake-
people disheartened, not thinking of the
tobacco farmer or the brown yards or
those like me who adore a gray summer
sky moving in low and full of grief,

a day when the woods are filled with dripping leaves.
Alone, quiet, heads leaned back, eyes closed tight.
Water against skin—that start when the two
forces meet—and then, sudden: the thick green
smell of life coming back. That scent, breathing

like mist on a June morning through the woods.
A straight-down rain, distant thunder grumbling
as it stalks up big-shouldered from the moss
banks of the Rockcastle, stomping like a
determined step-dancer over Slate Ridge,

shifting past Morgan's Branch and Pistol Creek,
churning off over Clay County, giving,
offering those little dry creeks a sup.
Deer and foxes might stir amongst the beech
groves, bend to have a drink. They too know what

it is to be lonesome. But it's only
the ground that has received water. I am
hopeless, in need of a good rain. Before
long I will be nothing more than the ghost
of a man, a Redbird River of rocks.

Couples

After seeing a Kennedy Center Performance of "Nur wer die Sehnsucht kennt"
with Renée Fleming, soprano, accompanied by pianist Evgeny Kissin

Only those who know longing, know what I suffer,
she sings in German, her voice a hovering bird.
Kissin plays the piano like rain falling
onto a green river. The music they make
is the air between bird and river, rising, falling.

Beside us, an old couple lean into one
another, fingers entangled. Their age is
defiance, every wrinkle a lived thing:
a kiss, a birth, a loss. While the great soprano
trills and the mesmerist sways and fortes,
the old man runs his thumb along her forefinger
and every stroke tells her:
> *I've loved you my whole life.*
> *Thank you.*
> *I don't want to go on living without you.*

Schubert wrote this piece for Goethe's poem.
The young composer understood pining,
recalled cold nights lying awake
in the same room
with his librettist, listening
to the lift and fall of his breathing.

Goethe's last words: *More light.*
Surely we are safe here, among all places, to
touch without fear, so I take hold of your hand.

The day we were finally allowed
to marry, there was dancing in the streets.
Now, once again, there is marching.
I run my thumb over your forefinger, ciphering:

Let us grow old together.
I am the river, you are the bird,
our bond—the air.

Northern Lights

I longed for you before I knew
you; that's what I always think
when something like this happens.
I never dreamt I would see them,
especially from my own back porch
right here in Kentucky. But there
they are. The richest purple, glowing
green, the blush of them,
an undulating mystery
as abstract as the enigma that brings
two people into the same orbit.
Here we are, watching them, together,
and we always will be, even when
we are nothing more than sky.

How I Had Church This Sunday Morning in July

I swept the kitchen floor,
neat little pile of dog hairs
and bread crumbs and grass tracked in

from the backyard. I thought of
my mother's blue-veined hands
on her wooden broom handle. She

believed and believed and she
believed that cleanliness was
next to Godliness but she

wouldn't sweep on the Sabbath.
I watched from the window as
my boon companion gathered

the morning's harvest from the
garden. He is strong-legged
and there is a prayer on

his face always. He carried
in six red tomatoes, one
yellow, and three cucumbers.

I held each of them, brushed the
black dirt away, a sort of
christening, knowing that they

were holy in their ripeness.
When the sun had come up high
enough for me to feel it

on the nape of my neck like
a punishment and a kiss
I took off barefooted,

went to the garden alone.
As I cut the zinnias
their musky green scent washed up

and I was drawn back
to a hot July morning in my
childhood, standing by Granny Mae

as she cut flowers and said,
I was a schoolteacher in Bright
Shade before I met your daddy's

daddy and destroyed my life.
Oftentimes she prayed
aloud in the hot damp fields.

While I washed dishes I thought
of my children, either still
asleep—red hair across

their pillows, their breathing loud
in a quiet room—or dressed
in uncomfortable clothes,

listening to the Holy
Roller preacher at my old
church. This evening when I

see them for the first time in
a week, I will put my lips
to their foreheads and let them

linger there. I believe I
will know the world is real then.
To drive away the grief I put

on a record. Nancy and
Norman Blake doing *The Fields
of November*. When Nancy

pushed her whole being into
that cello it was like
hearing God cry out

in joy and sorrow. You
can hear Him singing all the
time if you are very still.

Part II

New Year Prayer

Find a body of water, and be still
beside it for a time. Build a fire
and watch the flames. Sit on the porch.
Lie on the grass. Light candles. Take
a deep breath. Write a letter to
someone. Discover something new
everyday. Learn. Tell stories. Listen
to old people. Ask them questions.
Give to others when you can and treat
yourself occasionally. Read real
books and newspapers. Always buy the
grocery store flowers if they catch
your eye. Remember that there is power
in moderation. Learn to cook or bake
a new dish. Enjoy every meal. Savor
your food. Drink water. Any chance you get,
hold a baby. When the opportunity
arises, dance. Always swim or wade
in the water. Study leaves. At least once
this year, pee outside. Be completely
quiet. Turn your favorite song up
loud. Sing along. If someone makes you feel
bad all the time, get away from them. Laugh
with others. Laugh while you're alone. Spend time
with animals. Don't judge. Think this: "There but
for fortune go I" or "Everyone
you meet is fighting a hard battle."
Forgive others. Forgive yourself.

Those Who Carry Us

When I was little, a storm gathered
in the night with shivers of lightning
and quaking thunder. The rain fell cold
and sideways for three days. All the creeks
conspired to the raging river.
As the flood seeped beneath our door
my mother sat me on her hip.
> She carried me, muddy foam
> striking her knees, then her waist,
> before she reached high ground, where
> neighbors waited to help us.

Once, my aunt ran down the road with me
latched to her chest, a tornado
behind her. In the church basement
we could hear the havoc. She whispered:
If you are still and quiet this will pass.
> Afterward, a mighty moon shined
> so bright I could see our shadows
> as the world dripped and righted.
> Already people were rebuilding.
> Even hammers and saws make a kind of music.

Often, these days, I study
on those who carry us.
The everyday people who
keep the engine of the world
running. When the darkest skies
move in, I remind myself
that most people are good.

I think of schoolteachers who say:
You matter. Bus drivers who are glad
to see us each morning. Lunchladies,
laughing as they ladle out our food.

All those who stand up for what is right.
There are so many ways to change
the world. The mechanic and miner,
mail carrier, cashiers and clerks.
Singers, farmers, and truckdrivers.
      I can see them. I imagine
      their sore shoulders and tired legs.
      I thank them for carrying
      me, even when I didn't know.

We carry each other, from Pine Mountain
to the Pennyroyal. Past tulip
poplars and goldenrods. From city
streets to holler roads, from the wide
Ohio to the quickening
creeks of the Gorge, we go forward,
together. We lift our neighbors
from Hickman to Hindman, Mayfield
to Louisville, Cadiz, Cumberland Falls,
Falls of Rough, from the Bluegrass to Bowling
Green. Eminence to Independence.
Lawrence, Laurel, LaRue, I will carry you.
      Kentucky, we walk a ways together, no matter
      if it is in cold rain or moonlight. Sometimes
      the only music is hammers and saws, but we
      keep going, aiming for the high ground where they
      will be standing with their arms out, saying,
      Come here, and rest. Let me help you.

For You Who Have Loved Old Dogs

Old Andy is a big dog, black as a
night sky in the most lonesome winter months.
He is fat even though he doesn't eat
much these days. His man is one of the best
folks I know. They were hiking deep in the
high mountains when good Andy's back legs stopped
their work. The old dog folded himself down
on the path, his eyes lighting on his man's
to apologize. My friend carried him
nearly a mile, this great sprawl of blessed
animal, who must have lain in his arms
both thankful and ashamed. They collapsed
together at the end of the steep trail,
holding on to each other, exhausted.

I'm thankful for you who take care of old
dogs. I'm glad you have one another when
you need a friend the most, that you've had times
of stillness, watching the world, that you know
the grace of silence together. I thank
the infinite eternity and the
God of my understanding for people
like you, who carry them when they need you.

Three times now I've held an old dog
in my arms as they left me. Three times
I felt their heartbeats fade away on my palm,
witnessing a shooting star become
more darkness. The end. All is lost and gone.

I've grieved for each of them just as much as
I have for people I've loved. I've carried
the sweet sorrow with me, a heft I wish
I did not have to bear but one that I
will always cherish now. The burden
of my empty arms is the greatest weight.

For My Dog

I thought I might travel
to the Amalfi Coast this summer
but I prefer you, my little heating stove
at my feet, to the warmth of a
hundred Italian suns. I would
rather feel the rise and fall
of your breath beneath my hand
than all the bobbing boats of
Positano. What good is seeing
the Pietà when I can watch you,
watching me? The Trevi Fountain
has nothing on our little spot
down by our creek where you like
to doze while I read.

Don't Burn, Don't Fade

Remember that night in late summer
when we took a drive out in the country
before your veins were full of poison?
You always knew we had to live.

When we took a drive out in the country
you were speeding past Hurts Creek.
You always knew we had to live
with abandon, hungry for more.

You were speeding past Hurts Creek.
The Cranberries were cooing like doves
with abandon, hungry for more.
Still hot at midnight, the moon a scratch.

The Cranberries were cooing like doves.
Before we knew you were sick.
Still hot at midnight, the moon a scratch,
not bright enough to dim the stars.

Before we knew you were sick.
Before your veins were full of poison.
Not bright enough to dim the stars.
Remember that night in late summer.

False Spring

I saw the yellow first thing
this morning. Tiny petals,
peeping onto the warmth of
false spring. We have all these
little winters, you see. Just
when we think the worst is
over, sure as daylight,
we will have at least one
snow on the new blossoms. We
will be given a frost
warning. Daffodils, jonquils.
The cold will burn up the
startling brightness of our
forsythia but soon
the world will warm and the petite
leaves will venture forth: hopeful,
hopeful, like the dawn-time
warblers who sing to announce
they have made it through
the long night once again.

Double Creek Girl

They don't expect much out of girls
raised on Double Creek.
Up where the pines hang low
over the road like a tunnel
and the sun doesn't rise
until the rest of the world
has had its coffee and forgotten
the magic of morning already,

up where evening mist breathes
over the clean graveyard
and gardens with their straight rows.
They don't think girls from a place
like Double Creek will amount

to anything at all.
Especially when you were little
and they had pictures of girls
like you in all the magazines.
Life and *Look* and *Time*. Once,
a man from *National Geographic*

came and took pictures up there.
Girls in dresses their mothers made
and stringy hair, hollow-
eyed, hungry-eyed, sad-eyed.
But you defied them, Double Creek Girl.
You showed them. Every time
you opened a book and drank it up
like spring water. Each time you read

a poem and closed your eyes at the end,
savoring it like a good hunk
of cornbread, seeing it
like an azure sky, tasting
the words like the wet in a bloom

of honeysuckle. You showed them
when you listened to every word
the teacher said and walked
that commencement line and took
your degree from the hand
of the professor who was
secretly one of them. He never
thought you could do it. But you did.

See here, our Appalachia, our
bone and blood. Listen, our
Double Creek girl: You are
what happens when we know
that God lives in between
the pages of books and at the tips
of pencils and on the sharp
edges of notebook paper.

That's something they'll never know.

Pining

I have longed for you the way
A.P. longed for Sara,
the way he pined
and grieved himself to death,
walking those railroad tracks,
           his eye resting
on that mountain, his voice,
                once rich as coal,
quieted forever because he could not
have her for his own.

I have yearned for you the way
bluebirds must wait for spring,
when they can feel sunlight
warmth on their wings.
I've needed you like
old record albums need
needles, the way
displaced guitars
              hope for fingers
or unread books desire a pair of eyes.

I am the irises
              that grow
              beside the
              highway,
planted by a man with rough hands,
              ages ago.
He never imagined they'd one day
be forgotten. I am the shade
beneath the sugar maple
that people shun because they stay
inside on a summer's day.
              I am the call
of a whippoorwill no one hears.

I've waited for you until
I am a hollowed-out acorn
                        without its cap.
I have pined for you until I am
nothing but the thrum of hope.
I make no more noise
than the breath of redbirds.

North Fork

In the emptiness of night,
as rain pounded on the tin roof like cloggers,
music like thunder or thunder like warfare,
                            never-ending,
a sound she will hear on her deathbed
and all around her the water
rose, her mattress a drowning lifeboat,
her feet submerged in the murk
and her whole life afloat here, old
pictures and pillows, clothes and a suitcase,
the great-grandbaby's toys. The Bible and
her eyeglasses and the wedding ring quilt,
                    sinking, sinking.
Down, down the rain
                    unceasing.
The day has yawned into being,
gray as stormcloudy caskets.
She can hear all the creeks,
the outraged river, the mountains
washing away. She cannot stand
to think of her little dog, carried
off, and all the dogs. Surely
someone took the cows and
horses to high ground, but she
remembers they haven't had
animals in years, all that is long gone
and she thinks of the mudslides, the roar
the hillside made, the crashing of
the barn. They said half the houses
up this way were piles of lumber,
pinned against the bridge now.
She had heard
            the explosion of each one.
Most of all she is thankful
that so many of her people

have gone on, that they never lived
to see this. Because this place is no
more, her home is the past.

When the window breaks at first
She thinks the house has come unmoored
but they are hollering for her to get out
and now the water is up to her neck
so in her mind she goes back eighty years
when she was a teenager and they used
to swim in the North Fork
on the hottest summer days. She
                    slips into the unknown
                    and the ghosts
guide her, ease her past the jagged glass,
out into the pounding meanness that
pecks into eyes. She goes under, the current
                    clawing at her,
                    thrusting her
against the bridge.
                    Urges herself back
                    up, heaving breath.
Men in the boat are leaning over, yelling.
She wants them to hush. She wants
some peace and quiet. So she bursts
into the raging deluge, a swimmer
on a peaceful river of old days.

Leslie County

A song, sung to the tune of "Skibbereen"

O Daddy dear, I often hear you talk of Leslie County.
Her creeks and valleys green, her mountains of wild bounty.
They say it was a pretty place of honeysuckle smell.
O why did you abandon it, the reason to me tell.

O son, I loved my native land with every bit of my pride,
till they took the mountaintop and all that we had died.
You couldn't breathe the air to save ye life, the water it was nasty,
and that's the cruel reason why I left old Leslie County.

O, it's well I do remember that gray December day.
The company man and the sheriff come to drag me rough away.
I'd laid in front of the dozers to make them stop before me.
And that's another reason why I left old Leslie County.

Your mother too, God rest her soul, fell on the snowy ground.
She fainted in her anguish, having seen the mis'ry round.
She never rose but died and went to the land of uncloudy day.
She found a quiet grave, my boy, in dear old Leslie County.

And you were only two year old, oh, I hated to raise you elsewhere.
But I had to take us to a place where good folks would give us care.
I wrapped you up in my coat and fled in the night unseen.
I heaved a sigh and said goodbye to dear old Leslie County.

Ghost Garden

Before this was an island,
in the middle of a man-made lake,
back when this was farmland,
a woman in a haint-blue dress
stepped out of her back door
to plant a handful of daffodils.

Over the tarried years the daffodils
crept beneath the loam of this island,
quiet in their work. A cellar door
stood at the center of this lake.
Once there was a hanger and upon it a dress,
in a closet in a room in the house on this farm.

White clapboards protected the farmhouse
when cold rains battered the daffodils,
yellow revenants dressing
the farm that would become an island.
A passage to before this was a lake,
with nothing but flowers and a cellar door.

Only a ghost garden now, a door
into the past of a forgotten farm,
buried places now under the lake.
Each Easter there are daffodils,
unconcerned this is an island,
but recalling the woman in her pale dress.

In the spectral mornings as she dressed
she glimmered in the mirror on her door.
Often she was troubled by dreams of islands
yet she never yearned to escape their farm.
The hills were enough, the fields with daffodils.
She was dragged away when they made the lake.

So many were drowned by this lake.
That gauze of cloud is her faded dress,
but she lives on in the daffodils.
Her initials are carved on the door
and you can still hear sounds of farming
as waves sup at the edges of isle.

That's when the lake is black, gone is the door,
the dress spills over the haunted farm
and below the land always, silent daffodils.

God's Key

For wherever two or more are gathered in my name,
there am I in the midst of them.
—Matthew 18:2

She picks that banjo like a woman
reading Braille. Listen to the ancient
tones, those clucks and pops. She pats her foot
to the beat of stories waiting there,
in her fingers. *Belonged to my great-*
grandfather. She pauses, spreads one big
hand out over the worn skin. *Bird's-eye maple.*

She is an Appalachian from the
Middle West, a child of the plains who
had the mountains in her memory.
I miss Kansas sometimes. Her voice
is like a cool rain. *I miss the sky.*
And I think she pictures
that big blueness, those bruised clouds
swelling, the plum horizon of dusk,
stretched out like time. *I once saw seven*
thunderstorms, all in one day.

She tells us how she lost use
of her pointing finger. *A rabid cat.*
That simple. She studies her own hand.
Better to play with your middle one
anyway. She holds out her ruined finger,
beautiful in its inflexibility,
lovely in its inability.

Then she launches into another
song and we are all taken away
from this place, away from the war and
the badness we know lives in this world.
And all at once we are floating

right here, right now, in this holy place.
We are a family now, a people
joined by music, by words. *This one
is in D*, she says as she picks the
opening lines so we can join in
if we want. *This is in God's key.*

I believe God made the world for nights
like these, when we are safe with our kin,
with people who have mountain blood
in their veins, with banjo players who
speak poetry each time
they put their fingers to the strings.

Symbiosis

Where we
sat in a womb
of forest the shadow
of a leaf fell atop my hand.
My veins

so much
like those in the
leaf, they the delta of
river seen by a bird flying
a noon

sky. Blood
vessels the same as
a winter tree. A hand,
a leaf, a river, and a tree.
Our veins.

Quality of Life

Can you hear them
howling for you?
—Senora May

All over Puerto Vallarta the dogs
run wild. Mangy mutts lounge in the meager
palm shade and confident chihuahuas cross
intersections. A beagle climbs steep hills
in Zona Romantica. A beggar
goes to a bodega where he feeds two
pesos to a machine that spits handfuls
of dog food. He tosses the hard pellets
onto the greasy sidewalk. A woman
wearing turquoise rings fills a metal bowl
with cold water every morning by
her shop door. Back home, I see dogs jerked hard
by leads and locked in cages. I wonder:
is it better to be owned, or alone?

The Most Beautiful Words

gloaming home afloat
adrift whisper
eucharist scripture
ethereal mineral
obsidian mystery
murmuration undulation

mother father
God dog

Appalachia Ireland
green rain blue truth
iridescent radiance
resplendent ripeness
illumination luminescent
leaf-light dappled darkness
rhapsodic quixotic
elixir opulence

palaver pining
illicit forbidden
diaphanous poem
dancing thunderstorm

books words
woods music
sacred holy
hallelujah
alleluia
reckon fecund
moss lichen

felicity fidelity
friendship adore
enchant endear
mesmerize melancholy
celestial navigation
dreamer somnambulist

ocean riverbank
creek flowing
wildflowers wind
flora and fauna
halcyon lupine
solitude epiphany

Happy Hour

Sometimes it takes years to find ones who fit
like a soft jacket. If they're safe enough
in their own skin, they let you be yourself.

I never had friends like those I have now.
Always before, I had to watch myself.
Sometimes it takes years to find ones who fit.

Enough is as good as a feast, they say,
so keep a small circle of folks living
in their own skin; they let you be yourself.

By firelight, beneath rain, washed in woodsmoke,
along the mist-laden curves of highways,
sometimes it takes years to find ones who fit.

So let's shout *Cheers!* and *Sláinte!* all we can.
Whiskeyed and weeded, more often dead straight,
in their own skin they let you be yourself.

I will carry you if needed, and when
you want me to I will hush and be still.
Sometimes it takes years to find ones who fit
in their own skin. They let you be yourself.

Ghazal for My Daughter

Who cares about Ireland when my child is alone tonight,
far across the sea. I only wish to be home tonight.

Always this exception, forever this grief, blue heartache,
the desire to show her how the Dublin moon shone tonight.

How can I love the Liffey or wander Wicklow Mountains
when I carry this sorrow aching to the bone tonight?

I cannot stand the thoughts of her growing up while I am
far away. Or to feel the loneliness I've known tonight.

So now I watch her sleeping, fancied clear in my mind's eye.
To travel across space and time I must be gone tonight.

A River

A river runs through you, and it always
has, from the moment I first knew you
          until this one just now.
There's always been a little fire burning
on your pine-shady banks
and anyone who knows you
steps closer to be near its flames.
Even when your voice trembles
          and your hands shake
there is strength in your shoulders,
a belief in every word you choose,
a careful step, like a man strolling
the kempt rows in his bountiful garden.

          You know yourself,
          so only be yourself
          and do not fret, for if more
          could be like you, they might
          be free themselves.

People have always been drawn to you
the way they need to be near water,
to wade in your kindness and wash
in the calm tide. A river runs through you
          and it always has.

Timesickness

In the hot summer darkness
we took red lanterns to the blackest
parts of the garden, searching
for nightcrawlers we'd use on our trip.
The evening was loud with insects,
screaming as if in warning
          or celebration.

We fished quiet coves the next day
and the sweet air hummed.
Jesus-bugs walked the green waters,
blacksnakes slunk the rocky banks.
Sis put her hand on the back of my neck
and my mother kissed my cheek.

Both of them sometimes cried
without explaining why,
          looking out at the lake.
The past was always shimmering
in their hard and soft faces.

And beyond our trinity: a ghostly
circle of light, the ones who hovered
so near. Those who had passed
long before, but always anchored to us,
kept bright by the stories.

This evening I am out in the darkest part
of the yard with my little lantern, listening
closely to its comforting hiss even as
its thin flame threatens to flicker out.

Part III

When Times Are Dark

When times are dark
build a crackling fire
and gather good people.

The Varied Thrush

I strolled the frozen woods
while the city of angels burned
and the cabal was applauded
in the capital. The sun a gray eye
that watched it all. So many of us
felt the end's breath on our necks.

But then the whistle of a flute,
the high cry of life from the top
of a cedar. A round, squat thrush,
a migrant dressed in soot
and orange, bright-footed.
A refugee we flocked to see
and even hoped to keep.

Behold This Dreamer

And when they saw him afar off, even before he came near unto them,
they conspired against him to slay him. And they said one to another,
Behold, this dreamer cometh.
Genesis 37:18–19

They crept in on the long-legged night
like cryptids might, like monsters.
Springtime darkness fulsome, tremendous,
stretched out like time and quiet
quiet. He could hear the truck slicing
the blue gravel long before
its headlights washed the blighted pines.

The two women in the back of the king cab
leaned out with cigarettes smoking
and red mouths laughing. The music
a rumble inside, until they opened
the door, releasing fiddle
and guitar and Hank Jr. cacophony.
Didn't know the men up front.
Blue dashboard gloam showed set shoulders,
sullen profiles, both looking straight
ahead, not speaking. The women hollered
over the song *We're going*
to Kingdom Come! He didn't know why
they'd want to go after dark
but no matter. He had been lonesome
and alone as he was most
of the time, and now he wasn't. The pot
tasted murky and sickening. He
thought he could hear the weed
burning and popping but of course he couldn't
because they were all singing
     along now
     It's just a fam-lee tradition

loud, bottles held high, windows
rolled down, the cool April wind pummeling.
A jar of shine in his hands.
He savored, implored the liquor against the roof
of his mouth with his humming tongue.
The headlights shined on faded redbuds
and cliff-face, a yellow highway
sign: *Beware of Bears*. Too fast too fast
and they were thrown from one side
to the other, but the women laughed
and now a faster song, *Hurts
So Good*, and even in the chaos
he saw the passenger stretch
his arm across the back of the seat so
he could touch the driver's
shoulder. Quick, but fire flaring there, plucked
before anyone else saw.
He never told a soul, afterward.

Higher the winding road, dividing the black
hours he knew so well, these
abandoned nights of spring in the holler
too early for the little live
things to be singing yet, only the pitied
spring peepers in a mudhole
calling *We're alive we're here*, and quiet otherwise,
the night stretched out like ice,
like time, like the way always must
be if you escape the Lake of Fire.
A Natty Light in his hand, ice
cold, so known he drank in gulps, foam on his chin,
running in a rivulet
down his neck, a snake in his shirt collar.

      The brakes thrown on hard, sudden,
      doors kicked open four at once, then

the women wrenched him out. He
met the ground with a crunch of his spine,

the back of his head crashing
so hard lightning flared in his mind. Boots kicked
him and the women screamed
all the names he had been called his whole life
in the school hallways, at kitchen
tables, as he fled the belt, classrooms,
lunchrooms, even his own bedroom,
words that were always there. Words that started
with F had more power. Those
ending with T had more sting. This curse had
both and he felt its potent
puncture, each time, like the tip of a whip slicing
the skin on his legs and neck.

He conjured life, flailed and striked, tried to rise
but then his fingers were stomped.
Knuckles popped, bones shattered, pain
prompt in his armpit, the fist in his groin.
Dark figures above him
but beyond: the night sky, endless, the stars
so many they were a smudge.
The moon was a ghostly spent melon rind,
the trees leaned over to see,
crowding closer. More curses, the Fs and
Ts, again. A slap, a hit,
spit in his eye, then he felt the heat
on his face, heard the humiliation,
tasted the dribble creeping
into his mouth. He could only see with one
eye now and when he tried
to call out the bones cried in his jaw.

All four of them by the truck.
Throw him in the lake, or over the cliff,
throw him away. He stood
despite his broken leg, he dragged one ankle,
skin peeling on the pavement.
He trudged jaggedly, aiming for the woods.
Found the cliff's edge, felt the height twisting

in his gut as he sailed—arms spread—
over the cliff, his back breaking tree limbs
and against his face, the smell
of new leaves small as squirrel ears, the minty
breath of pines, then the ground,
      guh-thump.

Engine roaring, music alive
again, peel of tires, the silence only springtime
says, Easter sky behind the woods.
He slept and awoke, drifted and flew, his
mother whispering *Goodbye,*
the movie of her being carried
away. Little footsteps,
a sweet wild scent like sandy dens and creekbeds,
like nighttime, and with one good
eye he saw the fox looming, felt the tickle
of whiskers as it drew
in his scent, startled to attention, then
scampered, curiosity
quelled like the fire of a match, extinguished.

Alone again, waiting
delayed like he had been his whole life
for any way out, dreaming
his time would begin, when he'd be free of sin
like the fox, racing through briars
and low mast, brambles and burrs, but still,
nothing would touch him, not then.

Last Supper

Deep in winter as the gloom increased
the only color left was redbirds.
She cooked a great feast
that steamed up the windows
and warmed the entire house. Yet she was
the source of heat, standing at the stove,
stirring the soup beans, checking
the cornbread, turning the salmon patties,
slicing the onion. Even as a child I
was already grieving the passing of all I knew
and loved, as if preparing myself for
my older years of intense timesickness.
I had no way of knowing this would be
        our final communion.
Outside the snow was falling like feathers
and the cardinals were eating on the yard,
dozens of them decorating the white void.
She sat across from me and I lifted the
spoon to my mouth and just before
I took this eucharist I looked at her
and said to myself, *Remember this.*

Ghost

Grief never goes away. It might change shape but it
always has its teeth in you.
—Allison Moorer

Hours after she died I was shocked
to find myself in the kitchen floor, howling
in pain. I had never known grief could become
physical, something that lurks in your guts,
uncurls, and demands to be let loose.

Seven years later and sometimes her scent still
cuts the air. Cigarettes and Elizabeth
Arden Red Door perfume. Seven years later
and still I pick up the phone to call her. Seven
years later and I can't watch her on film. Her
presence in motion conjures too tangible
an absence. But I often put on the songs she
loved the most. "Night Moves" and "He Stopped Loving Her
Today." "Wild and Blue" or "Don't Let Our Love Start
Slipping Away." I want to wail the way
I did in those first days but I don't anymore.

Other times I dance, imagining her there.
Eyes closed, lost to music. I used to believe
in ghosts. These days, I don't. She would be one
if she could. She would jump out and scare me
if she was able. She'd throw back her head and laugh
with her mouth open before firing up a
Winston Light and savoring every draw
and exhalation. She would be a smoking ghost,
one whose only sound is the *critch* of metal wheel
on her red Bic. She only visits me

in my dreams, and there she does not talk. We walk
together along the lake bank. She bends,
chooses the perfect rock, skips it across the calm,
green water. The waves are so gentle I can't
hear them supping at the shore. The quiet we share
in these reveries is the opposite of lament.

Rivers

For Breonna Taylor

Not far from the water
your daughter was sleeping.

O Kentucky: you hurt me and you heal me.
You cut me and you stitch me.

Your mountain tongues, your bluegrass
tongues, your western tongue,
your Louisville tongues.

Lou uh vuhl
Louey ville
Louis ville
Lou uh vuhl

On the banks of the Ohio.
The Cumberland and the Laurel.
Red River, Green River, Big
Sandy, Russell Fork, Levisa
Fork. And then:
the twisting Kentucky River.

O my Kentucky. You
hurt me and you heal me.
You cut me and you cut me.

Not far from the water
your daughter was sleeping.

When you won't listen you won't
listen. When you holler and scream.
When your silence means everything.

You hurt me. You cut me
and I wish you loved me
as much as I love you. I would
not just stitch you. I would never
cut you to begin with.

But then you march in the streets
for her. Then you say her name.
Then you lay down in front
of bulldozers. Then you stand
up for your children. And you
take me in, again. Begin
again. You put your arms around
me and tell me you love me.
You show me when you stitch me,
your needle catching the light
of the blue moon, the thread
that runs so true, the salve
made of coal, and tobacco, whiskey.
The salve made of rivers.

Not far from the water
Your daughter was sleeping.

Prove it, right now. Love me
as much as I love you.
She was a Kentuckian,
so be the best of Kentucky.
Be the holiness of your waters,
holy still even when polluted,
even when secret, when wild,
when dammed, in the dark stillness
of the night when you can hear
them if you hush, and listen.

Ode to Sinéad O'Connor

You were right about
everything. I
remember the night
we watched as you
stood magnificent
in your rage, tearing
the picture of the pope
in two. The silence
that followed for five
seconds before the
furor roared to life.
Even then, I stood
by you. I loved you
when you felt alone.

One of your songs saved
my life. "This Is to
Mother You." The words,
a congregation
when I wandered alone
in the wilderness.
Only someone good
could write such a song.
I was nineteen when
your bald head became
famous. I loved you
from the beginning.
Now people say you
are crazy. You were a

divided country.
You were colonized.
But always you fought
back. My singing bird.
My red football. This
is a rebel song.
The music will do
its work. How about
you be you and I be
me. How about we
let you grieve way way
across the salty
sea, three babies, I
set you free, I set
you completely free.

Hazel Dickens

As soon as I heard she had died I looked
a mess of soup beans, studying hard
for rocks, let the beans slide over my
outstretched hand and into the cold water.
I lit the stove eye, plopped in a big glomp
of grease, salted like a hillbilly
does: a lot. I stood there a long while,
but a watched pot never boils. So I
will wait here by the window, watching
redbirds fly hither and yon on a stormy
Good Friday. Later, when we are eating
our soup beans (and sweet onions, fried
taters, chow-chow, salmon patties) we
will listen to Hazel singing "Black
Lung" or maybe put on her and Alice
doing "The One I Love Is Gone" and
there will be nothing else except
the silver sound of forks between us.

John Prine

He offered his hand,
looked us in the eye,
said: "Come on, let's go."
                              We stepped
into the shadowy living room
of an old lonesome couple.
His songs had flies buzzing in them,
men drinking whiskey under the moon crying,
swimming suits on the line, just drying. We'd
get in his car and go flying down to the
                              Green River.
Sometimes we shot empty
Coke bottles with our pistols. He taught
us to *fish and whistle*
as we rode into the gloaming
with all the car windows rolled down
and the radio calming.

When we felt so low
we didn't know
if we could go on, he sang
You've got gold in you
                              and we believed him.
So, we got up and lived again.
That's just the way the world goes,
he told us, and to *eat a lot of peaches.*
He taught us about *boundless love*
and *no ordinary blue.* He
convinced us to forgive, too.

Sometimes the tunes were jaunty,
often haunting, full of pining
                              or *illegal smiling,*
memories that can't be boughten,
paradise that can't be forgotten.

Always he was our friend, the one we
could depend on. Even though
we never met him, we knew him.

How do we thank someone who saved our lives?
We keep singing his songs.

Blood Harmony
(The Everly Brothers)

There was power in the blood and it surged forward when their daddy dug coal in the Muhlenberg mines. Legend has it no one ever shoveled more in a single day than he did. And before they became two of the best-known brothers in the world their family was singing and thumb-picking and tapping their feet to the music. They must have heard it in utero.

When you can sing like that—like the waters of two rivers joining forces, like mist touching leaves, like prayers drifting up, up—it lives in your bones and blood.

The confluence of their voices started in Kentucky. And in a car piled high with everything the family owned as it traveled the dusty roads to Chicago, then Iowa. Their sound embodied all of those people and places, but always there was Kentucky because once it lives in you it is a little light that never dims.

One day they sang together and the light burst forth from them and into our ears and it changed music forever. O, Lord, the sound they made together. That was the music of brothers, of Kentucky, of Muhlenberg. Not completely country, not quite the blues. Something special and new and so perfect that someone listening might put their arms out and take flight on the congruence.

This Is My Heart for You

First: Rain on the mountain, marching over the mountain
like straight-down ghosts made real once they pinprick
the surface of the water. A distant thunder
that could be mistaken for the blasting
they are doing over yonder where another
mountain is being hauled out one piece at a time.
     You can see an entire entity passing beneath
     your feet if you pause on the bridge above the tracks.
But here, on this bridge, Troublesome churns underneath
us, brown and foamy. All the other little
creeks have ganged up and poured off the cliffs and hillsides
to their great way out, good old Troublesome
O Troublesome O Troublesome O good old creek.

2.

Turn on the faucet next morning and out comes
the water orange, the color of earth
that gets trapped way way down in the metallic
rocky canals that hide within the clefts
of mountains. O secret secret O holy
holy these places are, little hidden
spaces only known by God. We are a people
used to our water being tainted, for don't we
live in just such a world every determined
day of our lives when our mothers are telling
us we are not like them and our fathers
are yelling and waving pistols and all the world
says no, you are wrong wrong wrong very wrong.
But here, on Troublesome, we are of one mind,
of one family, and perhaps the creek
is our mother, maybe the mountain is
our mother. The black gum and sycamores
they comfort us, the red fox who comes out during

the sermon is our kin. Lord Lord Lord
what lurks among the gloaming's cedars,
watching us as we go about our busyness?
The wise old woodlanders sit back and they are pleased,
amused by our honesty that knows
no bounds here yet is tucked away in a little
box made of leaves when we are in the places
we call our homes but are not, really.
Otherwise we would not love this haunted place so much.

3.

Do Lord O Do Lord O Do remember me
the woman sings and we do we do we remember
remember remember. We are all memory
and remembering. This is my heart for you.
We are holding on with white knuckles and we mourn
for what we have not been able to clutch, we mourn
and preserve it and make it into poems
and songs and books and jars of pickled corn
we can sit on the windowsill to catch the light.
You cannot put back a mountain but you can
carry its stories strapped to your back like medicine bundles,
you can make a tattoo of them
on the underside of your arm. You can sew them
onto the unseen parts of your mouth. This is my
hand for you, outstretched, unfolded, unclenched—
everything but uncertain. Read them
the way the wise old-timers read the leaves
and the skies and wooly-worms. Read them and tell me
what you see in our past, in our creek,
on the side of our mountain. There is language
in the kudzu and it is all ours and belongs
to no one else. This is my tongue for you,
whispering our history: words words words.

4.

All week long the rain came and went, as did the stories.
Sometimes all would be as still as the voices
of sleeping birds, the leaves breathing against
the wooden shingles of the chapel, the graves
all wet and mossy. Not many mornings
were the spiders able to build their webs
in the corners of the bridge for the rains washed
them away. But always there were the words
and the songs and a thousand different kinds
of joys and griefs. All the while the people were singing
and the creek was running and the mountains
were breathing their last breaths and the kudzu was growing,
just waiting for the moment when it would overtake
every little bit of it, but the people
there cherished it anyway for it was their symbol,
the kudzu. Kudzu, kudzu, a word they sang
and claimed like their own although it came across the sea,
just like them, just like the vine itself. All
things that take up residence must first travel
and find their own secret places in the waiting world.

Night Watch

When the blue hour conjures
the world belongs
to insects and the moon, to cooing
birds and the possum,
who is watching by the creek.

I am the only one awake,
and while some may savor
the silence, I fear
there is nothing else.
The world is full of wild things
in cages. They keep me
up at night, yet my troubled
mind does not assuage them.

I am haunted by a donkey
I saw in Mexico,
made to stand for hours
in front of a tequila kiosk.
He looked me in the eye
as I strolled by.
Maybe he is happy,
my husband reassures me later.
Yes, I venture.

Perhaps in Puerto Vallarta
they have gone home now
and someone feeds him
sweet oats, pets him while
he drinks his fill.
I hope, I hope,
as the western sky lightens,
and day begins
once again.

Conversation With My Friend
the Morning After the 2024 Election

Weary times ahead, I say.
We'll make it through this, she sighs,
   and have joy along the way.

The New Regime

A darkness drops again, but now I know.
—William Butler Yeats, "The Second Coming"

To survive:
Sometimes you dance on the porch
or you cry on the kitchen floor.
I've howled in grief before and
if it helped I'm still not sure.
Put on the kettle, brew the tea.
Stir the stew and we'll visit some more.

To survive:
Watch closely, listen with a cupped hand
and when you come, holler loud
to let me know. If you moan
it feels better. If you're quiet
they'll kill you and no one
will even know. Be still,
always fight back, keep moving.

To survive:
Don't pick the flowers but
slip your feet in the creek.
Don't turn on the light or
they'll see us inside. Shine
bright enough and you'll blind
their snipers. If they tell you
you're crazy show them
that you are. Like a fox.

To survive:
Be cunning but kind,
be shrewd but never mean.
Be a knife that is sharpened
each time they cut you but
keep the meat of your heart
tender. Be aware. Watch closely.
Do not truck in empire.
We need no kingdom for the
power and glory are ours, forever.

Sundays

The bells and birds compete to testify
a new morning while grief pins me again
to the bed. This Sunday shares a sacred
lonesome when all the world seems at peace, and
quiet. Witness this day a wide darkness,
as all Sundays are full of harm for small
beings, whether sparrows or those who make
music and pick out their own clothes. Couples
stroll in their best and break bread together,
just the way it should be. But there is no
sabbath for dogs and the winged things, nor
those who find holiness in cedar trees
or slant of light. O love, please protect us.

Interview with Barbara Kingsolver

Silas House and Barbara Kingsolver grew up a couple hours from each other but met after both of them had become established in the literary world. They have been friends for about twenty years and share a deep love for the natural world, literature, dogs, and much more, as well as sharing a mutual respect for each other's work. What follows is their conversation about All These Ghosts.

KINGSOLVER: A lot of us know you as a novelist, and obviously you also write poetry. But your creative range also extends to plays, screenplays, short stories, creative nonfiction, journalism, music, and even music videos. Do you feel this versatility expands the reach of what you can do and say with your writing?

HOUSE: I feel like one form feeds another. I learn something from each thing I write, but I think poetry has taught me, more than anything else, the power of language. Writing poetry has made me think about every single word I write in a sentence of prose, too. Poems are hard and wonderful because you have such a small canvas, whereas novels are hard and wonderful because you have such a large canvas. I think writing of any kind should be difficult if it's going to be any good, so I never think of writing any of it as fun, but I do think of completing any piece of writing as enormously satisfying.

KINGSOLVER: Is there one genre that feels most like home to you, or is every project a fresh start?

HOUSE: Secretly I've always felt like a poet, even though, as you rightly pointed out, I'm better known as a novelist. So, I think I always had a deep desire to study poetry more intently, the way I have over the last few years, even though somehow I was always able to share my fiction more easily.

KINGSOLVER: To linger a bit longer on poetry specifically, what do you find appealing about this form, as a reader and a writer?

HOUSE: For one thing it is the challenge of saying something memorable in a very small space. And it is interesting to me that poetry is widely accepted as the oldest form of literature, yet it is so compatible with the modern world. There are studies showing that people have much shorter attention spans than they used to, mostly due to the internet, news sound bites, and the like, so a poem is perfect for contemporary people who may not feel like they can sit down and be moved by a novel but they can read a poem and have their day reshaped by it. So there is a lot of power in the form right now for that reason.

KINGSOLVER: I think all Appalachians are tired of outsiders getting us wrong. So I'm grateful to you as an author I reliably depend on to represent our home with respect, beauty, and authenticity. I also love the sense of pride that comes through in so many of these poems: "First Home" is a moving love song to a trailer home. "At the Opening of *Coal Miner's Daughter*" marks an exact moment of understanding that we are an "us." In your poem "Blood Harmony," for the Everly Brothers, you write, "always there was Kentucky because once it lives in you it is a little light / that never dims." Words like these make my own Kentucky heart beat a little stronger. Do you think artists have a duty to representation, whether that means geography or nationalism or identity, or whatever? If so, what is it? Are Appalachians a special case?

HOUSE: Well, first of all, thank you for these kind words. I was seventeen when your first novel came out, and to know you were raised so close to me and had this acclaimed book gave me permission to try to be a writer, too. So to hear this from you means so much. And I think that writers like you, Wendell Berry, bell hooks, Lee Smith, and others from the region set that example of not only being a writer, but also being a representative. I do think that people from this region have a bit more expectation to represent, because when you're from a place that the whole world has so many stereotypes about, when you're in the public eye you are more aware of those, and you want to correct them. When you're from a place that the whole world is telling you to be ashamed of, you react in one of two ways: you either have deep shame, or you have intense pride. I think most of us choose the pride, but that doesn't mean we only talk about what's good about the place. We tell the truth about it, and therein lies the complexity, which is of course the opposite of stereotype. One of our jobs is to complexify the people and places we're writing about, so really I think if a writer is producing good work, then that complexifying of the place happens.

KINGSOLVER: I love the physical specificity of these poems. Poetry naturally tends to be auditory, but these are also visual, tactile, olfactory—they call up all the senses. Here's an example of a line I picked out to savor, about rain coming after a drought: "A straight-down rain, distant thunder grumbling / as it stalks up big-shouldered from the moss / banks of the Rockcastle, stomping like a / determined step-dancer over Slate Ridge." I can see that, hear it, smell it, even feel it in the step-dancer's pounding rhythm. As I was reading these poems, I thought of an audacious question. We who live in the country are so closely entwined with the rich world around us, as we farm and garden and fish and swim in lakes, living our lives in the company of trees and birdsongs. Do you think this might give rural people a kind of poetic superpower?

HOUSE: I think when you live in a rural place or even if you live in a city and you consciously seek out the natural world, your life is richer, more centered, better. Yes, absolutely. And so I do think that gives us a kind of poetic super-power. I was a rural mail carrier for seven years, and although that's the hardest job I've ever had, it is also one that taught me the most about the natural world. In our daily lives if it comes a thunderstorm, our natural inclination is to run and get out of it, but as a mail carrier I had to stay out in it and deliver that mail, so I got to know the world during a storm in a whole new way. Similarly, I couldn't get in out of a very cold or very hot day like we would normally try to do. . . . I had to experience it, and doing so gave me a much deeper understanding of weather and nature.

One of the things I'm most grateful for is that I grew up in the country and that I was able to roam, wild and free. We spent whole days in the woods, in the creeks, on the riverbanks, climbing rocks, lying in the grass. Even now, I live in Lexington, which is a big city for Kentucky, but I chose a piece of land that has old trees and a creek, two big porches. We let about half of our yard grow wild so that we have more birds, more lightning bugs, more night sounds. So I will always miss living in a rural place, but I have created ways to foster it and live in it fully as much as I can. That makes me feel better, so that makes me a better writer.

KINGSOLVER: On the subject of rural life, the darker side of the coin is that we can feel cast out of our home for being different. One poem that really got to me was "Double Creek Girl," with the lines, "They don't expect much of girls / raised up on Double Creek / . . . You are / what happens when we know / that God lives between the pages of books." I grew up a far cry from Double Creek, but even so, I didn't have friends who loved to read or wanted to go to college. I felt continually warned against the abstract high-mindedness of being an artist, writing poetry, or even avidly reading it. We weren't supposed to "get above our raisings."

HOUSE: Same here.

KINGSOLVER: Likewise, in "Little Fire," "Cumberland Falls," and many others, I could feel the intensity of your experience of growing up gay in the midst of people, including your own younger self, who didn't quite understand what that meant. The risk of losing your community is so deeply felt, in a place where community is really everything. Can you offer some thoughts on how you've processed that in your work and your life?

HOUSE: Yes, that's a big theme in this book, loving a place that you don't always feel loves you back as much, and that's mostly because of the legislation being passed and the way people vote in this region. I don't necessarily think that there's any more bigotry in Appalachia than anywhere else, but I certainly notice it there more because it's where I'm from, and I should feel safe and welcomed in my home. At the same time, even if I know bigotry lives everywhere, I can look to the way a place votes and see that validated in different ways, so it's troubling and hard to rectify, especially when I know the people to be so loving. It's a constant heartache for me, but of course that gives me more to write about, and it gets to that complexity I was talking about earlier. We should seek to not romanticize a place just as much as we seek to not vilify it. Simplification lives in either. And so I'm glad you're seeing the light and the darkness in this book; I really wanted to show both, and I wanted to tell the truth about the place. I think that's important, and even dangerous to not do so.

KINGSOLVER: A recurring motif I recognized here is the family story: a father's baptism, an aunt's poignant tableau of blue glass. A mother who was orphaned at ten, waiting for your quickening in her belly that finally made her whole. There's something irresistible in the idea of a whole, perfect story, polished to a high shine, complete in a single page. Would you say that narrative poems have a special claim on you, and if so, what is it?

HOUSE: Absolutely. As someone who was trained primarily as a prose writer I've had to work hard to find the balance of being a narrative poet and not just a novelist writing a poem. So I've strived to find the most precise imagery, to prune and polish sentences, to find the music in the lines in ways that poems can do but prose cannot. I love trying to conjure an entire world and characters in a very small space and using poetic devices to bring them alive.

KINGSOLVER: Formal poetry gets more than a few nods in this collection: there's a beautiful little shaped poem called "Watch Closely," about small things. There is the sestina called "Ghost Garden," and also a pantoum in "Don't Burn Don't Fade." I know you read a lot of poetry, both contemporary and classic, and that songwriting also interests you. So I wonder, in a modern world, what do you think we can we gain from the classic rules of line, stanza, rhyme, and form?

HOUSE: I love writing poems using strict forms. It forces me to really put my nose to the grindstone on the language. It makes me think much more deeply about word choice, rhythm, all of it. And honestly, I am a person who loves formality in a world that increasingly rejects it. I put great store by decorum and rules. A lot of creative writers really cringe at the idea of rules; they think they hem in creativity. But I tell my students that we must know the rules in order to know how to break them. And sometimes those rules exist for good reasons—like making our writing better.

One of the hardest poems to write in this book was "Ghazal for My Daughter" because the ghazal form requires a lot of repetition, which I tend to avoid in most of my writing. But I was determined to use that form because that poem is all about separation, and ghazals, an Arabic poem form, most often focus on being separated from someone you love, so it felt like the perfect form for that poem, which is about missing my child when I was overseas.

I really like to play with how poems look on the page, too, but I do that pretty sparingly in this collection. The two most obvious ones are that in "Ode to Sinéad O'Connor" the stanzas are arranged to look like the Irish flag and in "First Home" each line is meant to look like a trailer and its porch since the poem is set in a trailer park. But there's also "Three Sisters," where the stanzas are arranged to look like the trio of diving cliffs and the lines in "Dale Hollow Lake, 1989" are indented to create a similar shape to waves. Most readers might not even notice that but if they do it gives it a deeper meaning.

The worry, of course, is that it might seem old-fashioned to use these forms, but the poem wants what the poem wants. Perhaps nothing conjures *old-fashioned* more than outright rhyming, which I only do in one poem, but it's the opening one, "Lost Place," because it is an homage to A. E. Houseman's poem "XL," which examines the same themes in outright rhyme. I was worried about opening with that poem because I feared readers might think the whole collection was going to be rhyming, but my editor convinced me that it worked and established the theme of the book so well that we should lead with it. I think she's right.

But overall I think this is one of the reasons to be a poet, to play with these forms and challenge oneself in these ways.

KINGSOLVER: The first poem after the prologue, "Gloaming," sets the tone for the book beautifully. There's so much of home in it, so much memory, and also the sense of a lost time we can't get back, even though the gloaming is that moment of perfect stillness between daylight and darkness when time seems to stop. I'm not sure how I know this, but I've known for years that *gloaming* is your favorite word. And sure enough, later in the book, it stands at the head of a poem called "The Most Beautiful Words." Do you love that particular word because this poem was always inside it for you? Or is it the opposite—this poem was an exploration of what you could find in the word? Or maybe some combination?

HOUSE: That's such a beautiful question. Thank you for that, and thank you for listening so closely in our conversations that you know my favorite word. I grew up around people who were often using words that the rest of the world deemed archaic, but even as a child I knew these words had great value and I felt a sense of duty in preserving them. I think that's one of the main reasons I became a writer, really, because I knew the rest of the world discounted these words and even thought they were low-class or ignorant. It reminds me of what my friend, the poet Jane Hicks, has pointed out: if a British person uses the word *reckon* then most of the world thinks them elegant, but if an Appalachian person uses *reckon*, most of the world thinks they're stupid.

About *gloaming*, though, I believe it is the first word I remember hearing and thinking that it perfectly captured what it was describing. That specific moment of dusk when there is a certain stillness and even a particular quality of light, that moment that feels somehow sacred if you take note of it. And the word just sounds exactly like that with the softness of the *gl* sound, then the way the word stretches out with that long *a* and eventual landing on the softness of the ending *ing*, which has been made gentle by the preceding letters and sounds. I know, I'm nerding out on this word, but that's what writers *should* do. And this book is so much about the concept of timesickness that I think *gloaming* is a pretty perfect way to conjure a place in time because it's about stillness and quiet.

KINGSOLVER: Do you feel your engagement with words and language is different in poetry than when you're writing fiction?

HOUSE: Oh Lord, yes. And I think that writing poetry has made me a better fiction writer. When we are taught fiction, we are instructed more stridently on things like characterization, sense of place, dialogue, propulsion, but I believe we should spend just as much time centering our minds on the language, on word choice and rhythm, all of those elements that are more commonly associated with poetry. Of course in a poem you have to do it more frequently and be much more aware of it because of the economy of a poem.

KINGSOLVER: "New Year Prayer" I plan to print out and tack to the wall beside my desk. This poem contains a marvelous wisdom, all the way to its parting kiss: "Forgive others. Forgive yourself." I also found enormous resonance in this line from "Cornbread: "This is the curse of who we are / as a people, always eating / our own history, tasting the past." And in the simple, elegant pronouncement in "Those Who Carry Us," that "there are so many ways to change the world." And in this poem for John Prine: "How do we thank someone who saved our lives? / We keep singing his songs."

HOUSE: I can't thank you enough for reading the poems so closely.

KINGSOLVER: We may think we're looking for entertainment or escape when we turn to literature, but really I believe we're looking for wisdom. A writer needs to do some serious living in order to write something worthwhile. You've been creating beautiful work for decades, and I assume these poems are also the work of many years. But there's something in this collection as a whole that landed for me in a way that felt new. Do you feel this book marks an arrival of a different kind of maturity in your career?

HOUSE: Well, I think part of that is just reaching a different level of maturity overall. Since turning fifty I have seen everything so differently. I'm not sure I have any kind of wisdom, but I do believe that I've learned a lot from my mistakes, and the older I get the more I can look back and see that I should have reacted differently to things, that my own actions often led to bad outcomes. So it's all a learning experience. I have never been able to separate "real life" from my writing; it's all the same thing. And I think one reason that there may be some kind of feeling of wisdom being shared in some of these poems is that the current moment leads me to think a lot more about empathy, about how easy it actually is to be good to others, to just let people be. When writing lines like "Forgive others. Forgive yourself," I'm writing that to myself as much as I am to readers. I'm not so much sharing wisdom as I am reminding myself that this is the best way to be.

KINGSOLVER: You've just spent the last year as Kentucky's Poet Laureate, and when I look at the schedule of events you've kept, it makes my head swim. You are clearly committed to expanding public understanding and appreciation of literature and poetry, which is another whole vocation alongside of being a working artist. I want to thank you for everything you've done as a writer, and also as a teacher and ambassador for literature.

HOUSE: Well, I learned from writers like you and Lee Smith and Adriana Trigiani and others that as artists we are also representatives, whether we want to be or not, and that as public figures we have a duty to our people to serve them the best we can. And that's just a big part of our upbringing as Appalachians, I think. You have to do for others. You are expected to pass on the good that was given to you.

KINGSOLVER: How do these two vocations connect, add to each other, or subtract from each other?

HOUSE: I'll return to the word *empathy* here. As writers, we must try to understand the motivations of every character—even the antagonists—and I think that helps us to think more complexly about everyone, even those who seek to do us harm. One thing I tried to do as poet laureate was represent as many people as I could and to make them all feel heard and seen. I feel like I have many different facets—not just one—that allow me to understand a wide range of people. A lot was made of me being the first openly gay poet laureate of the state, and one of the only ones ever in the South; some of that was positive and some was very negative. But I am much more than that. I am also someone who was raised lower working class in the trailers of Appalachia. A lot of people have thanked me for being vocal about that. A whole lot of people are raised in trailers or love people who live in trailers, yet when trailers are discussed in popular culture it's almost always to criticize or belittle the people who live in them. So I was really proud to be out there complexifying the lives of those people by talking about my experiences of living in trailers. I'm a vocal person of faith who is also liberal and gay, and I think it's really important to talk about the idea of there being a Religious Left when all we hear is about the Religious Right. Liberal people of faith exist, too. I'm also first gen, meaning I'm the first person in my family to graduate—or even attend—college. My point here is that visibility matters, and it was one of the great honors of my life to get to represent this large swath of people as I went around spreading the word about literature.

KINGSOLVER: How do you see the artist's responsibility to outreach and accessibility?

HOUSE: To me that's part of being an artist. Some people disagree and they hide away and do their writing and put it out into the world and that's it. And that's fine; I'm not judging that. But for me, being an artist is about being accessible. Often being a working writer is like being a juggler. I am often overwhelmed and burnt out by it, but I'm also reenergized by meeting people and hearing their stories, and there is nothing better in the world than when a reader tells you that they've been moved or changed by your work. For me, I am writing for that one person who will gain something from reading my writing. That's my audience, that one person. And this book is for them.

ACKNOWLEDGMENTS

Appalachian Review: "At the Opening of *Coal Miner's Daughter*, Corbin, Kentucky, March 27, 1980," "Double Creek Girl"
Ghost City Review: "Night Watch"
Gravy: "Cornbread"
Kudzu: "Sis, 1956" (published as "She Moved Through the Fair")
Lexington Herald-Leader: "Those Who Carry Us" (this poem was also published in a broadside by October Press and Larkspur Press)
Motif: Writing by Ear: "God's Key"
Now and Then: "Drought"
Red Branch Review: "First Home," "His Body, Appalachia," "Cousins"
Salvation South: "Gloaming," "For You Who Have Loved Old Dogs," "When Times Are Dark," "Ghost"
South Writ Large: "Northern Lights," "For My Dog"
Still: The Journal: "Only Thing He Ever Gave Her," "Rivers"
The Bitter Southerner: "Cumberland Falls"
The Louisville Review: "Lunchlady," "Couples," "The Varied Thrush,"
The Southern Humanities Review: "Behold This Dreamer"
Untelling: "My Mother, Orphaned at Ten," "Three Sisters," "Porches, Early 1980s"
We All Live Downstream: "Leslie County"
"Easter 1954" appeared in a slightly different form on *Pine Mountain Sessions* (album).
"Hazel Dickens" was originally published as a broadside by Holly Hill Restaurant.
"John Prine" was originally published as a broadside by October Press.
"Little Fire" was originally published as a broadside by Carnegie Center for Literacy and Learning.
"This Is My Heart for You" was originally published in the play *This Is My Heart for You* (Berea College Press).

My deep thanks to all of the editors who originally published many of these poems, especially John Compton, Kyle Tibbs Jones, Jeremy Paden, Chuck Reece, Flora K. Schildknecht, Noah Soltau, and Marianne Worthington. Your belief in me as a poet has made all the difference.

I am grateful to Lynn York, Robin Miura, Arielle Hebert, and the entire team at Blair for being such a lovely group of people to work with. A true pleasure during the entire process. A special thank you to poetry editor Sandra Beasley for making this book better with her keen insights.

I am indebted to poetry mentors Jane Hicks, Lisa Parker, and Marianne Worthington, who have patiently taught me so much about the craft. I am grateful to Barbara Kingsolver for encouraging me to pursue poetry. Friends made at the Appalachian Writers Workshop and the Naslund-Mann Graduate School of Writing have been invaluable to me in learning the craft and finding community. I'm thankful to Alice Hale Adams for giving me honest and quick feedback on many of these poems. I cannot express my appreciation enough to David Arnold, Gavin Colton, and Johnny Lackey for always listening.

I was fortunate to have parents who encouraged me to read and write, and a lifelong friend who has been reading poems to and with me from the beginning: Donna Conley Birney.

I could not write anything without Jason Kyle Howard, the first to hear each poem, the opinion I value the most.

NOTES

"Couples," "Northern Lights," "How I Had Church This Morning in July," and "Pining" are dedicated to Jason Kyle Howard.

"Lunchlady" contains a nod to and was inspired by Robert Hayden's "Those Winter Sundays" and is dedicated to my mother.

"Those Who Carry Us" was written to commemorate the second inauguration of Kentucky Governor Andy Beshear and was delivered on the steps of the Kentucky State Capitol on December 12, 2023, at the inauguration ceremony.

"For You Who Have Loved Old Dogs" is dedicated to Johnny and Jenny Lackey, in memory of Andy.

"Double Creek Girl" is for Sylvia Woods.

"God's Key" is dedicated to Sue Massek.

"Happy Hour" is for David Arnold, Gavin Colton, and Johnny Lackey.

"Ghazal for My Daughter" is for my daughter, Cheyenne.

"A River" is dedicated to my son, Levi, and is influenced by the song "A Feather's Not a Bird" by Rosanne Cash.

"Timesickness" is for Lisa Parker.

"The Varied Thrush": In early January 2025 a varied thrush was spotted in Lexington, Kentucky, more than two thousand miles from its native habitat on the western coast of the United States, where wildfires were ravaging Los Angeles. By Inauguration Day dozens of birdwatchers had descended upon the neighborhood where the bird was visiting. While the subject of this poem did make me think of Thomas Hardy's "The Darkling Thrush," it borrows none of that poem's form, lines, or themes. This poem is for Jane Hicks.

"Behold This Dreamer": On April 4, 2011, in Harlan County, Kentucky, four people lured a young gay man into a truck, took him to a deserted road in Kingdom Come State Park, and beat him nearly to death while screaming bigoted slurs. When they paused to discuss how to dispose of him, he escaped by jumping off a cliff. The four were later charged with the first federal hate crime in the nation. All of them were prosecuted for assault, but the jury acquitted the accused of the hate crime charges even though one confessed the attack was motivated by homophobia.

"North Fork": During the late July 2022 flood that hit Central Appalachia, a photograph of ninety-seven-year-old Mae Amburgey sitting on her bed as waters overtook her home in Whitesburg, Kentucky, went viral and made national headlines. She survived the flood when rescuers broke out a window and she swam out on her own to an awaiting boat. She passed away only three months later. "I believe she died of a broken heart," her granddaughter, Missy Amburgey, told *The Lexington Herald-Leader*. "I think if it hadn't been for the flood . . . she would have still been with us."

"Ode to Sinéad O'Connor" is arranged in the shape of the national flag of Ireland, frequently referred to in Ireland as "the tricolour," or *trídhathach*.

In "John Prine" the italicized lines in the poem are lyrics from his songs. "John Prine" was commissioned to commemorate the dedication of a statue of John Prine in Central City, Kentucky, and read onstage at the Ryman Auditorium for the third annual John Prine "You Got Gold" Celebration.

"Blood Harmony (The Everly Brothers)" was written for the dedication of a statue in their memory which was erected in Central City, Kentucky, in 2024 and was read at the ceremony.

"This Is My Heart for You" is for Marianne Worthington.

"Night Watch" is for Nicholas Alexander Brown Cáceres and Christopher Neuhaus.

"Conversation With My Friend the Morning After the 2024 Election" is for Shaina Goodman.